Guitar
Rock Songbook

INTRODUCTION

Welcome to FastTrack™!

Hope you are ready to play some hits. Have you and your friends formed a band? Have you and your friends formed a band? Or do you feel like soloing with the CD? Either way, make sure you're in tune and comfortable… it's time to play!

As always, don't try to bite off more than you can chew. If your fingers hurt, take some time off. If you get frustrated, put down your guitar, relax and just listen to the CD. If you forget a technique, chord, or note position, go back and learn it. If you're doing fine, think about finding an agent.

CONTENTS

ABOUT THE CD

Each song in the book is included on the CD, so you can hear how it sounds and play along when you're ready.

Each example on the CD is preceded by one measure of "clicks" to indicate the tempo and meter. Pan right to hear the guitar part emphasized. Pan left to hear the accompaniment emphasized.

ISBN 978-1-4234-9571-0

7777 W. BLUEMOUND RD. P.O. BOX 13819 MILWAUKEE, WI 53213

Visit Hal Leonard Online at
www.halleonard.com

LEARN SOMETHING NEW EACH DAY

We know you're eager to play, but first we need to explain a few new things. We'll make it brief—only one page...

Melody and Lyrics

The additional musical staff on top shows you the song's melody and lyrics. This way, you can follow along more easily as you play your accompaniment part, whether it's chords or harmony or a blazing solo.

And if you happen to be playing with a singer, this staff is their part.

Endings

1st and 2nd Endings

These are indicated by brackets and numbers:

Simply play the song through to the first ending, then repeat back to the first repeat sign, or beginning of the song (whichever is the case). Play through the song again, but skip the first ending and play the second ending.

D.S. al Coda

When you see these words, go back and repeat from this symbol: 𝄋

Play until you see the words *"To Coda"* then skip to the Coda, indicated by this symbol: 𝄌

Now just finish the song.

That's about it! Enjoy the music...

❶ Are You Gonna Be My Girl

Words and Music by Cameron Muncey and Nicholas Cester

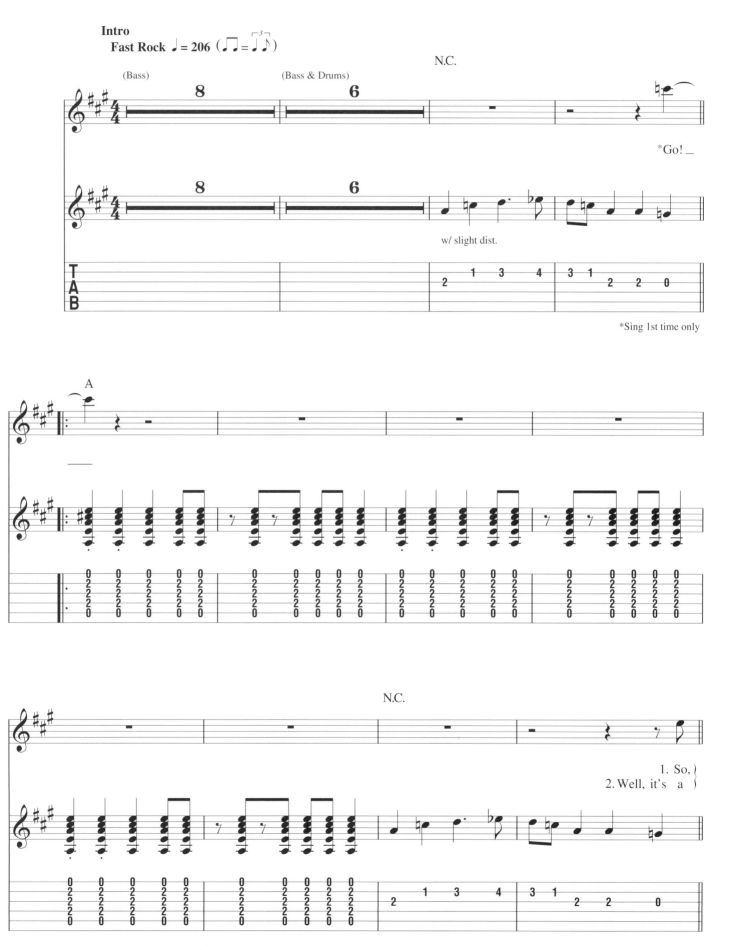

Verse

one, two, three, take my hand and come with me be-cause you look so fine and I

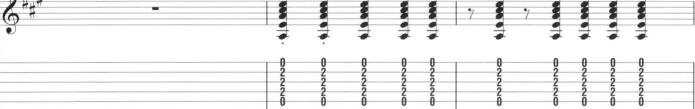

real - ly want to make you mine. I say you

look so fine and I real - ly want to make you mine.

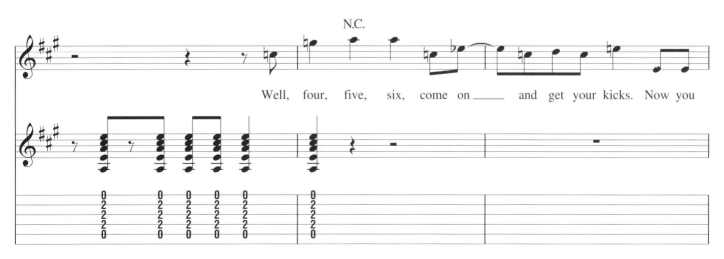

Well, four, five, six, come on _____ and get your kicks. Now you

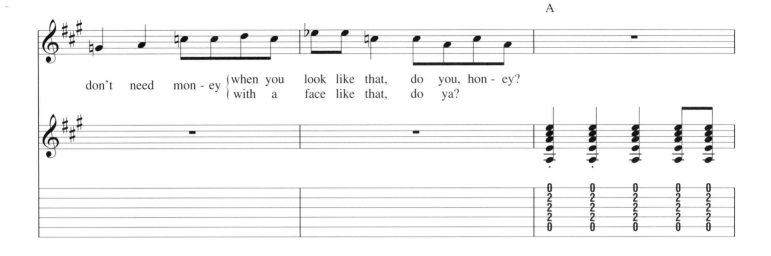

don't need mon-ey {when you look like that, do you, hon-ey?
{with a face like that, do ya?

N.C.

Pre-Chorus

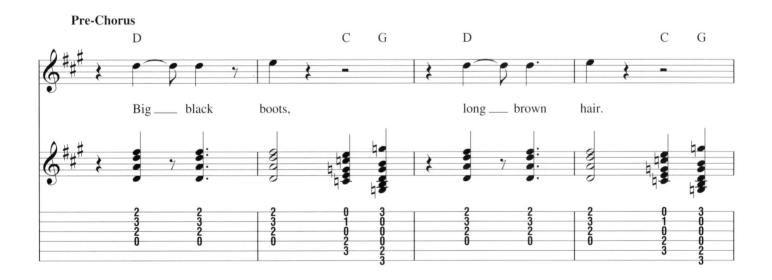

D | C G | D | C G

Big ___ black boots, long ___ brown hair.

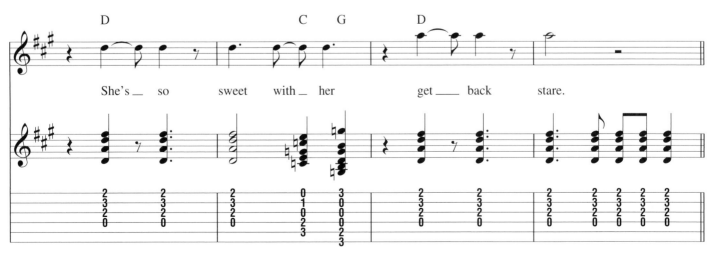

D | C G | D

She's ___ so sweet with ___ her get ___ back stare.

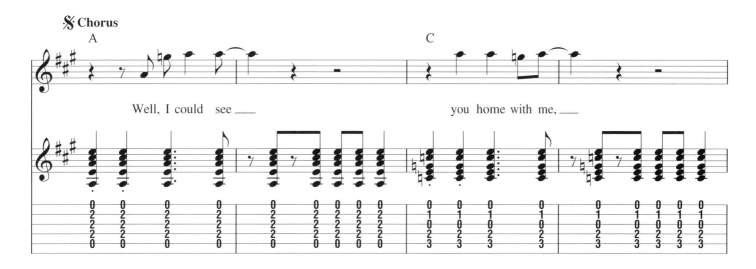

Well, I could see ___ you home with me, ___

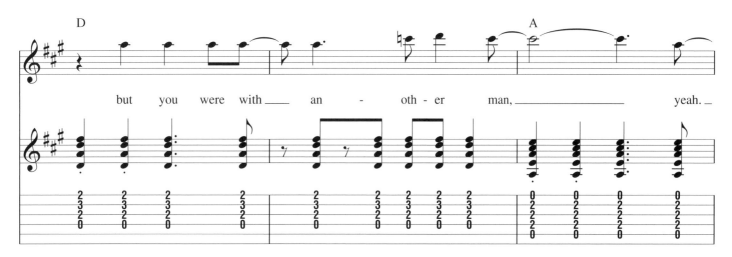

but you were with ___ an - oth - er man, _____ yeah. ___

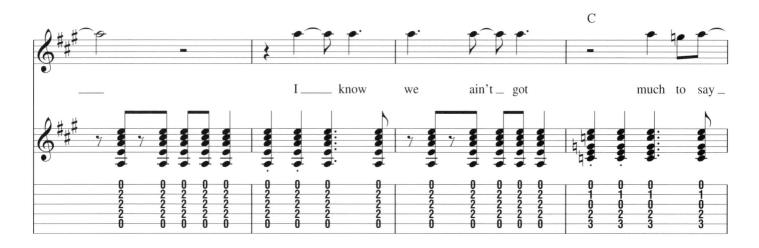

___ I ___ know we ain't ___ got much to say ___

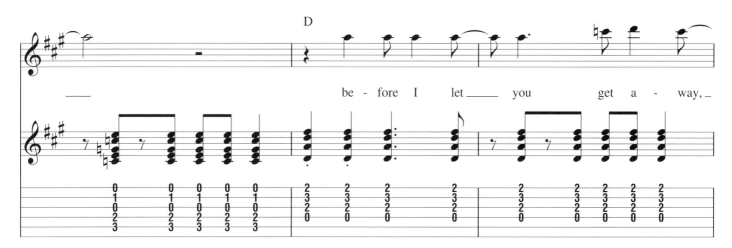

___ be - fore I let ___ you get a - way, ___

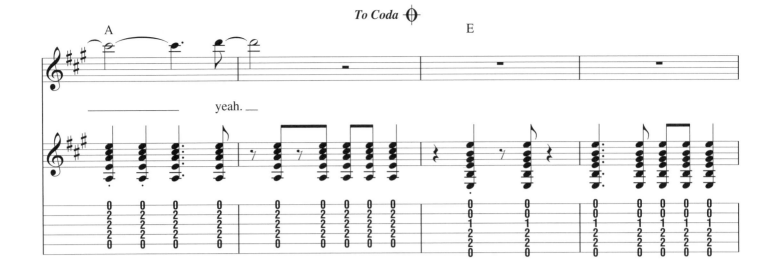

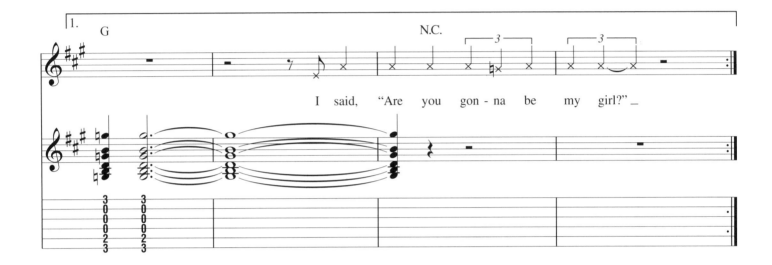

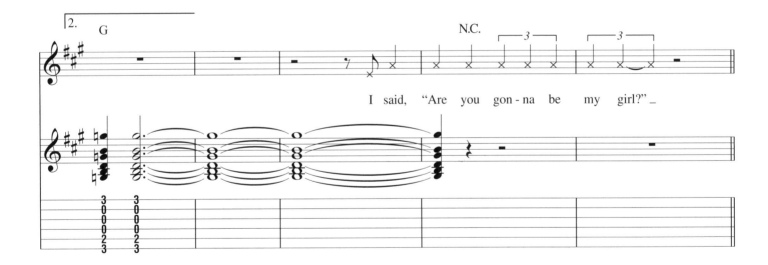

Interlude

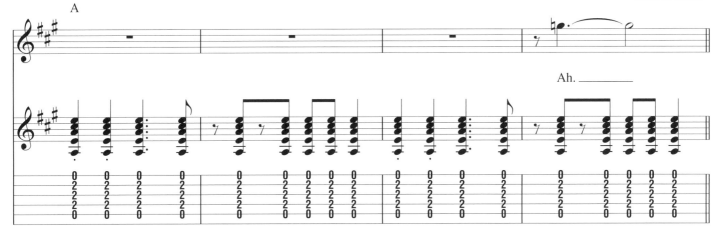

Ah. _____

 Coda

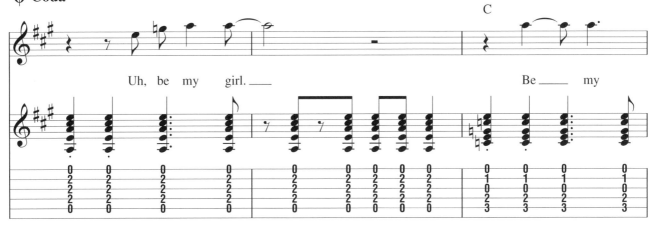

Uh, be my girl. _____   Be _____ my

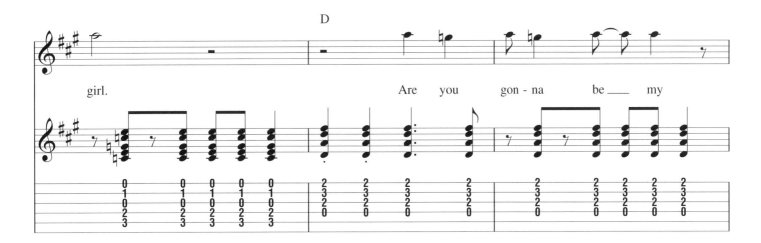

girl.   Are you gon - na be _____ my

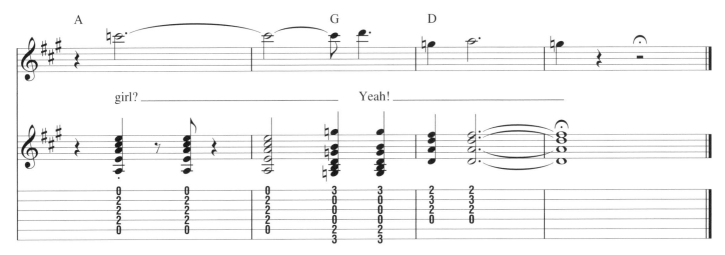

girl? _____   Yeah! _____

❷ Clocks

Words and Music by Guy Berryman, Jon Buckland, Will Champion and Chris Martin

Intro
Moderately fast ♩ = 132

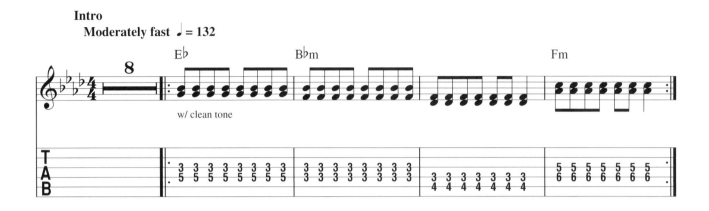

w/ clean tone

Verse

1. Lights go out and I can't be saved. __ Tides that I tried to swim a - gainst __
2. Con - fu - sion ____ nev - er stops. __ Clos - ing __ walls and tick - ing clocks __ gon - na

Quietly during Verse

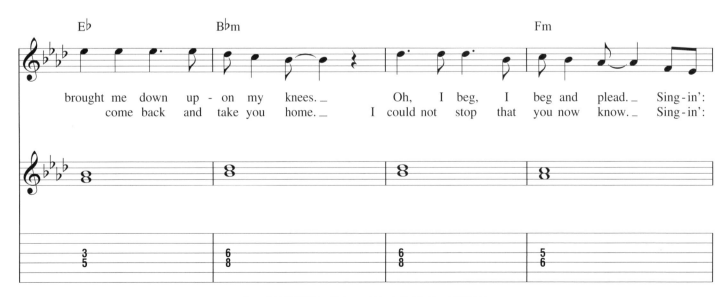

brought me down up - on my knees. __ Oh, I beg, I beg and plead. __ Sing - in':
come back and take you home. __ I could not stop that you now know. __ Sing - in':

come out of things un - said. _ Shoot an ap - ple off my head. _ And a
come out up - on my seas, _ curse missed op - por - tu - ni - ties. _ Am I

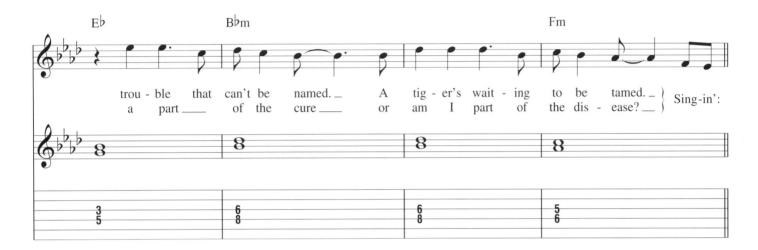

trou - ble that can't be named. _ A tig - er's wait - ing to be tamed. _ } Sing-in':
a part _ of the cure _ or am I part of the dis - ease? _ }

Chorus

You _____ are. _

To Coda ⊕

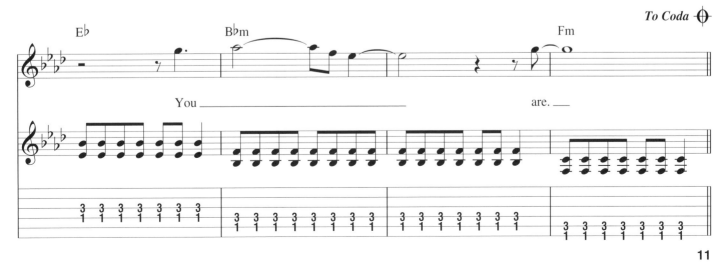

You _____ are. _

Interlude

2nd time, D.S. al Coda

⊕ Coda

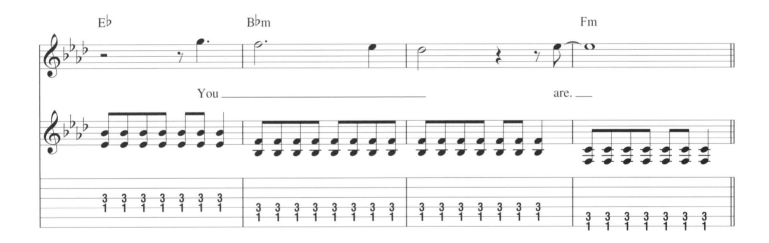

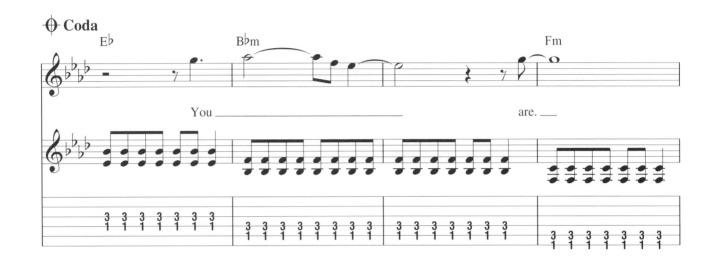

Bridge

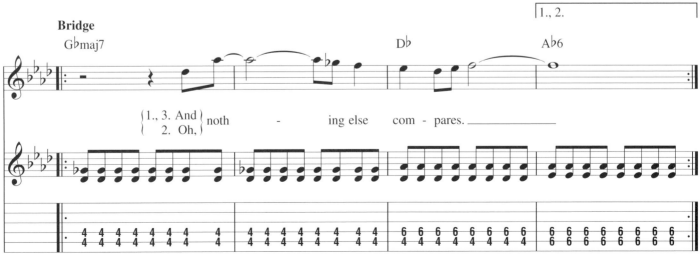

12

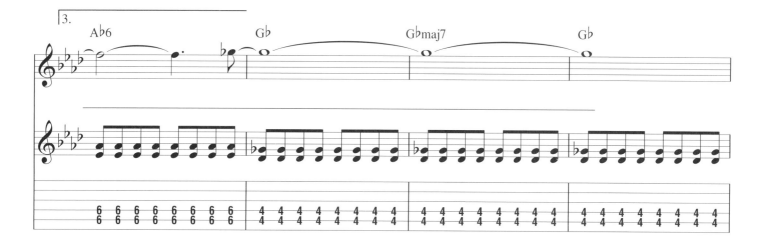

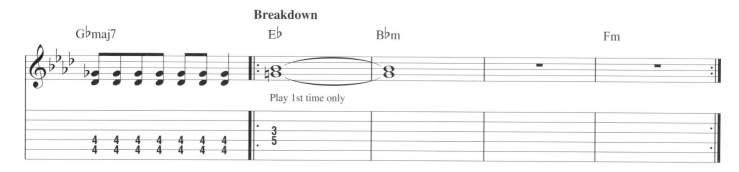

Breakdown

Play 1st time only

Interlude

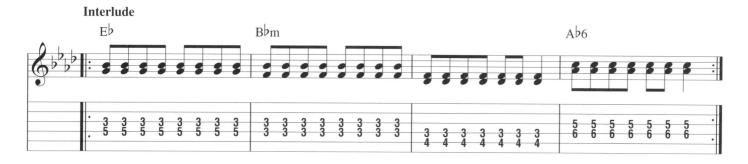

Outro

Play 4 times

Home,   home, __   where I want - ed __ to   go.

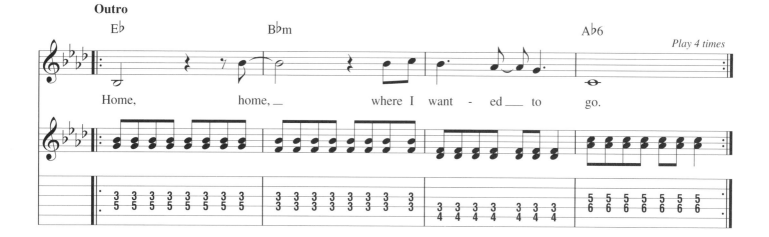

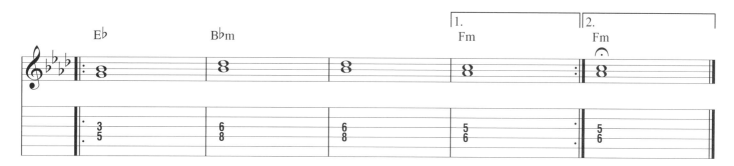

❸ Dani California

Words and Music by Anthony Kiedis, Flea, John Frusciante and Chad Smith

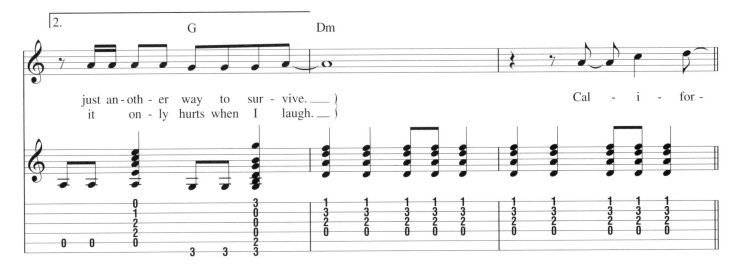

Chorus

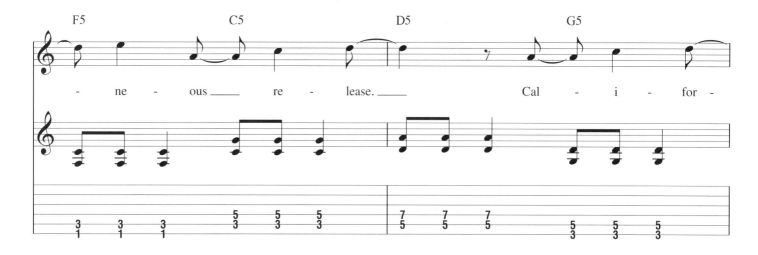

-ne - ous ____ re - lease. ____ Cal - i - for -

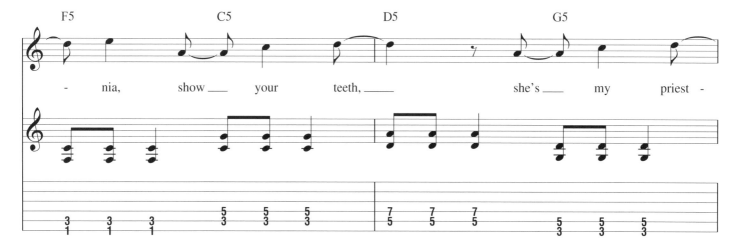

- nia, show ____ your teeth, ____ she's ____ my priest -

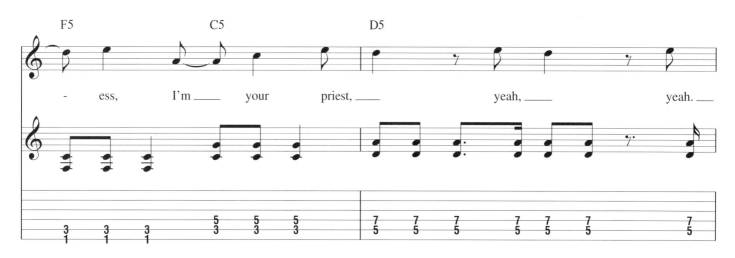

- ess, I'm ____ your priest, ____ yeah, ____ yeah. ____

To Coda ⊕
Bridge

____

Who knew the oth - er side ___ of you?

Who knew what oth - ers died __ to prove? Too true to

D.S. al Coda
(take 2nd ending)

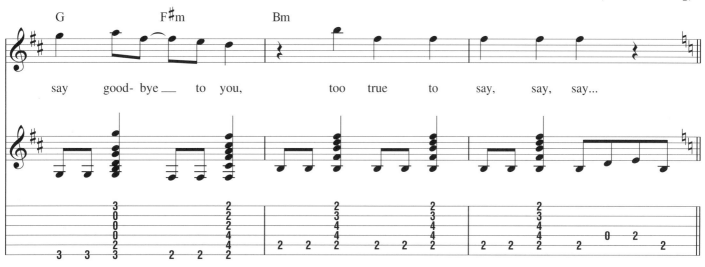

say good- bye __ to you, too true to say, say, say...

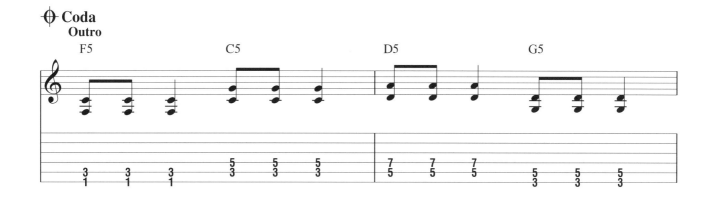

Coda
Outro

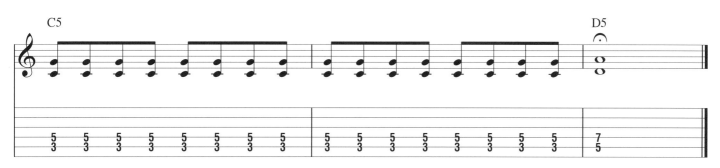

17

Gives You Hell

Words and Music by Tyson Ritter and Nick Wheeler

you're still prob - 'ly work - ing   at a nine to five __ pace. __
nev - er seemed __ so tense, __ love.   I've nev - er seen you fall so

hard.   When you see my
And do you know where you

Chorus

face, hope it gives you hell, hope it gives you hell.   When you walk my

way, hope it gives you hell, hope it gives you __ hell.   2. Now, are?   And

Guitar begins
w/ clean tone

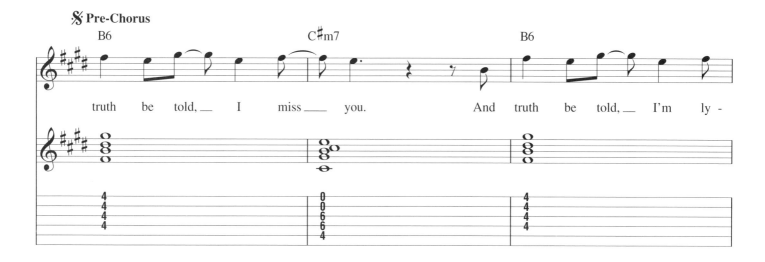

Pre-Chorus

truth be told, __ I miss __ you. And truth be told, __ I'm ly-

Chorus

ing. When you see my face, hope it gives you hell, hope it gives you

w/ slight dist.

hell. When you walk my way, hope it gives you hell, hope it gives you __

__ hell. If you find a man __ that's worth a damn __ and treats you

To Coda 1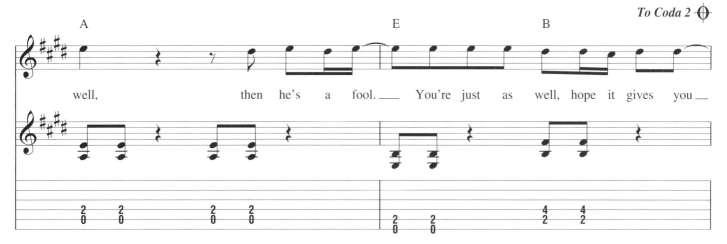

To Coda 2

well, then he's a fool. ___ You're just as well, hope it gives you ___

Interlude

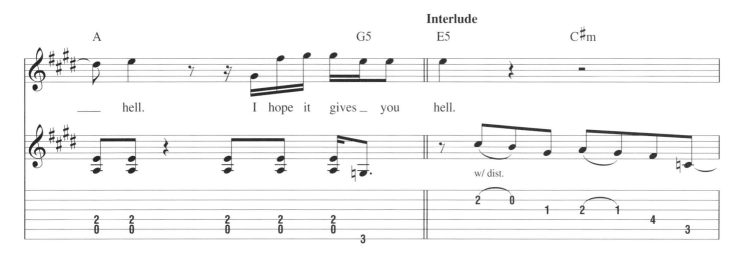

___ hell. I hope it gives ___ you hell.

w/ dist.

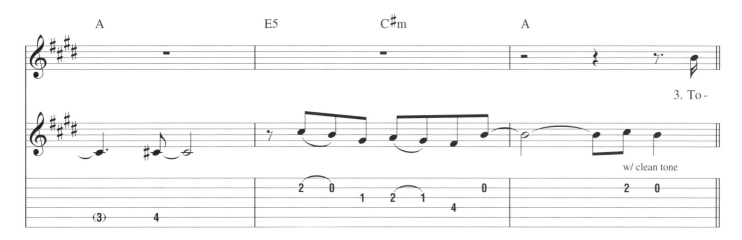

3. To -

w/ clean tone

Verse

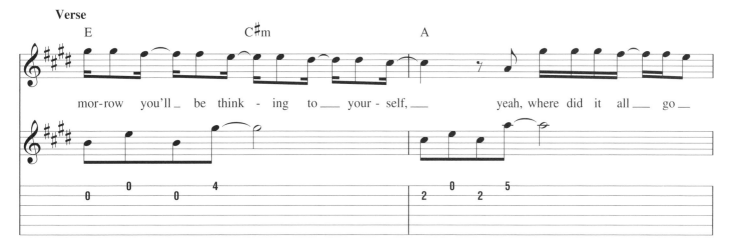

mor-row you'll __ be think - ing to __ your-self, ___ yeah, where did it all ___ go ___

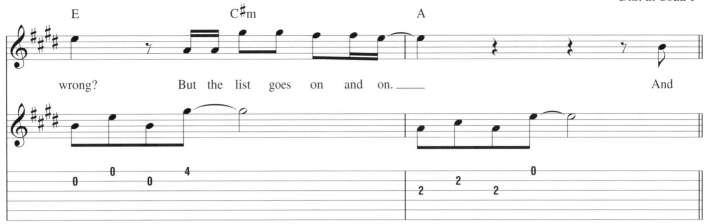

wrong?   But the list goes on and on. _____   And

Coda 1

_____ hell.   Now, you'll nev - er see _____ what

w/ clean tone

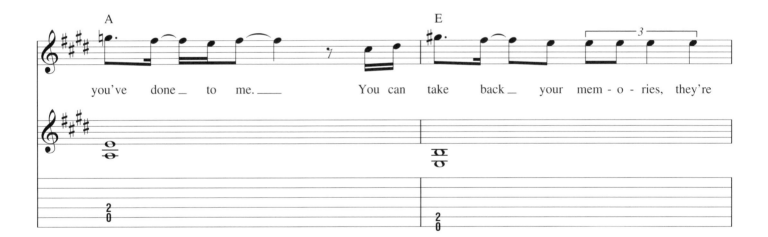

you've done _ to me. _____   You can take back _ your mem - o - ries, they're

no good _ to me. _____   And here's to all _ your lies, _ you can

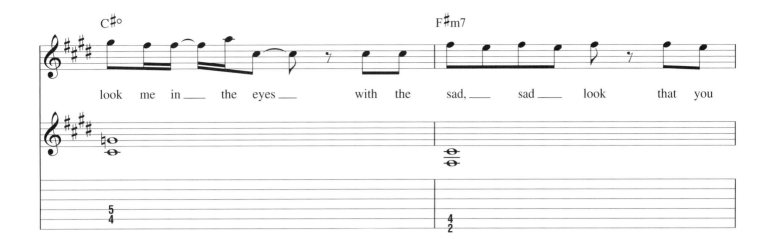

look me in the eyes with the sad, sad look that you

D.S.S. al Coda 2

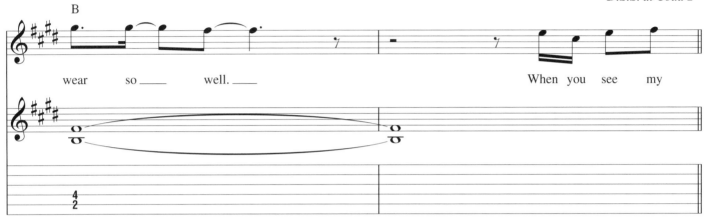

wear so well. When you see my

Coda 2

Outro-Chorus

hell. When you see my face, hope it gives you hell, hope it gives you

hell. When you walk my way, hope it gives you hell, hope it gives you

_____ hell. When you hear this song and you sing a- long, __ but you nev- er tell, __

_____ then you're the fool. I'm just as well, hope it gives you
song, I hope that it will give you

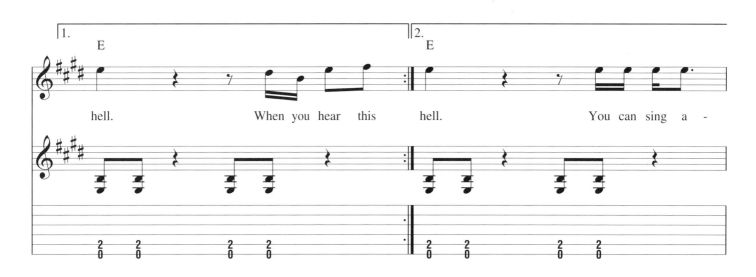

1.
hell. When you hear this hell.

2.
You can sing a -

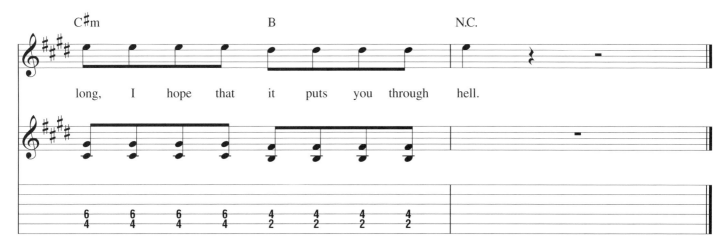

long, I hope that it puts you through hell.

Grenade

**Words and Music by Bruno Mars, Ari Levine, Philip Lawrence,
Christopher Steven Brown, Claude Kelly and Andrew Wyatt**

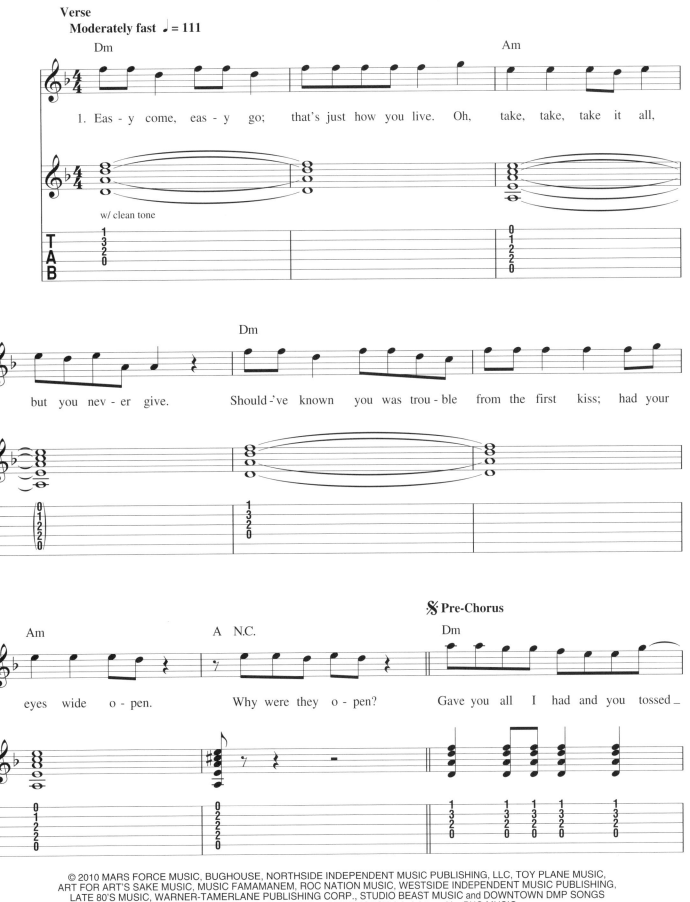

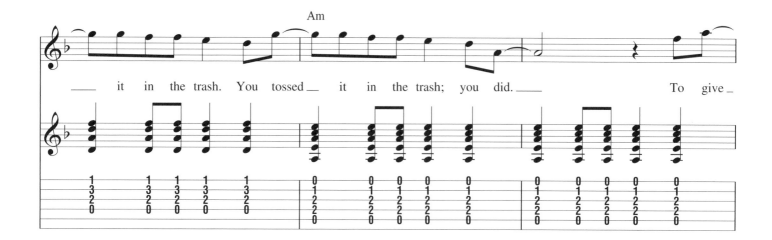

_____ it in the trash. You tossed _____ it in the trash; you did. _____ To give _____

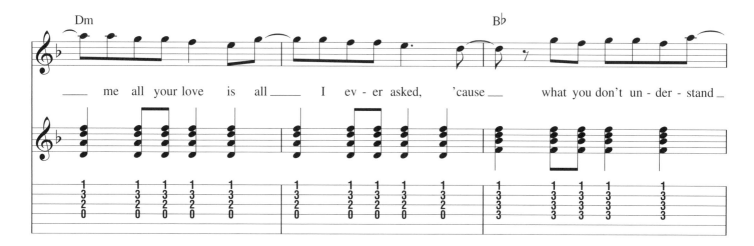

_____ me all your love is all _____ I ev - er asked, 'cause _____ what you don't un - der - stand _____

𝄋𝄋 Chorus

_____ is, I'd catch a gre - nade _____ for ya, _____ throw my hand on a blade _____ for ya.

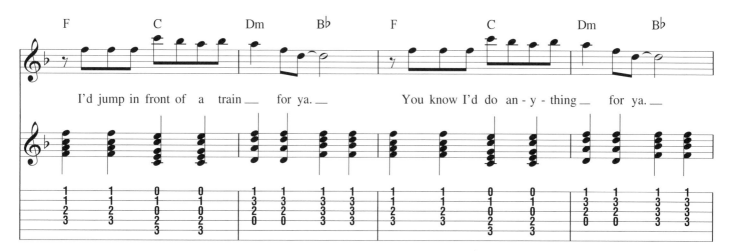

I'd jump in front of a train _____ for ya. _____ You know I'd do an - y - thing _____ for ya. _____

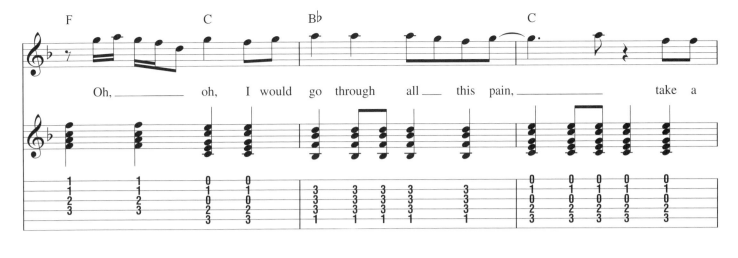

Oh, _____ oh, I would go through all __ this pain, _____ take a

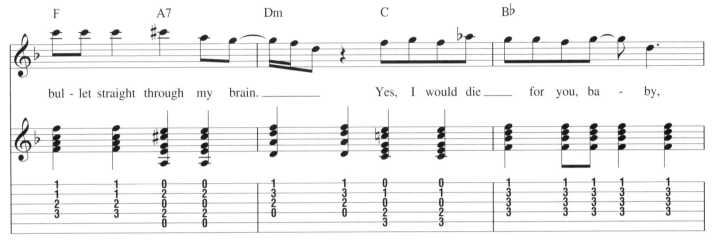

bul - let straight through my brain. _____ Yes, I would die __ for you, ba - by,

To Coda 1 ⊕
To Coda 2 ⊕

Interlude

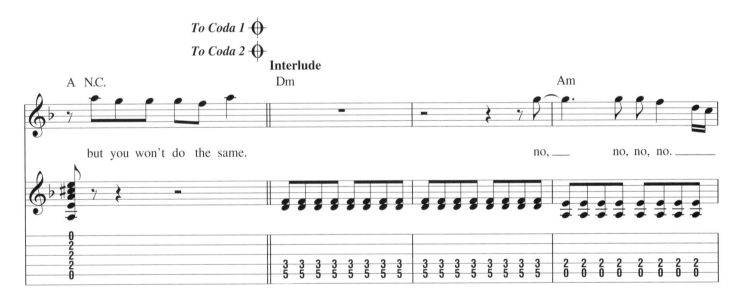

but you won't do the same. _____ no, ___ no, no, no. _____

Verse

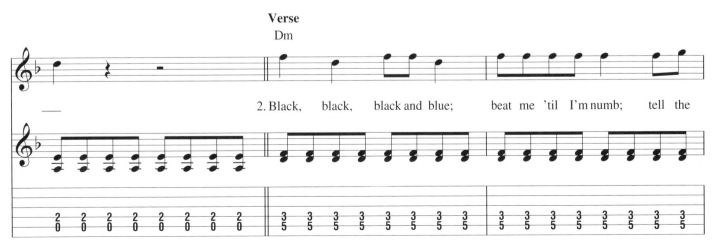

2. Black, black, black and blue; beat me 'til I'm numb; tell the

dev-il I said, "Hey," when you get back to where you're from. Mad wom-an, bad wom-an;

D.S. al Coda 1

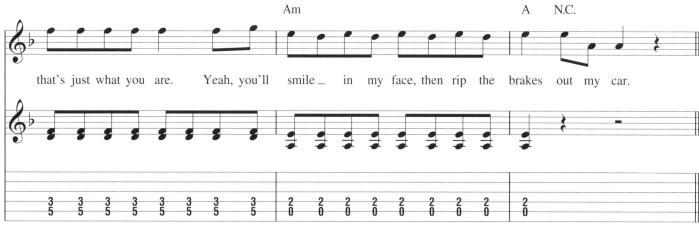

that's just what you are. Yeah, you'll smile __ in my face, then rip the brakes out my car.

⊕ Coda 1
Bridge

If my bod-y was on fi-re, ooh, you'd

watch me burn down in flames. You said you loved me; you're a li-ar, 'cause you

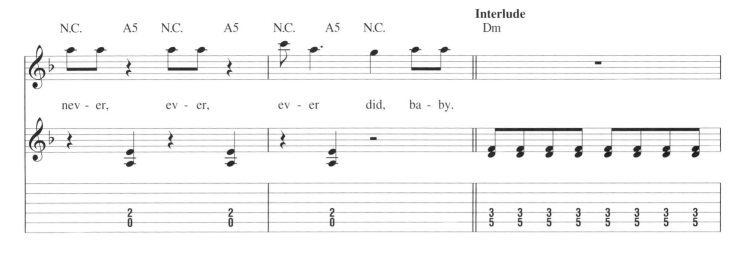

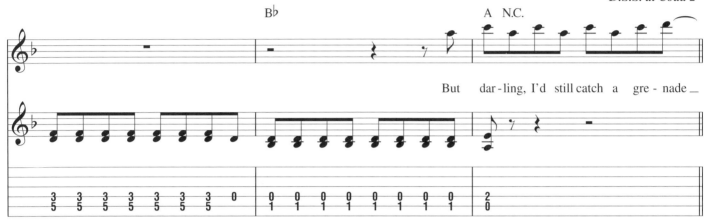

Home

Words and Music by Chris Daughtry

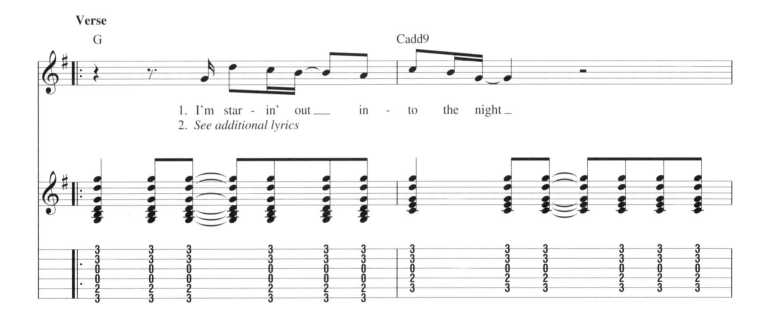

Intro

Moderately slow ♩ = 72

w/ clean tone

Verse

1. I'm star - in' out ___ in - to the night ___
2. *See additional lyrics*

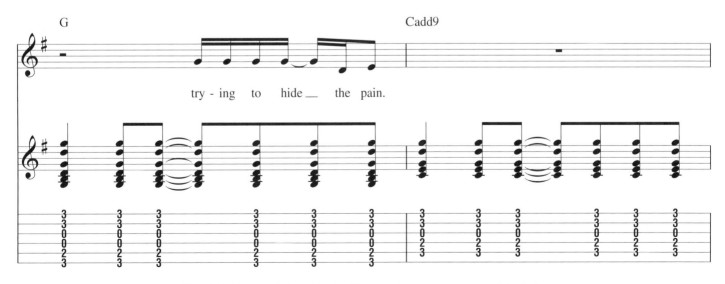

try - ing to hide ___ the pain.

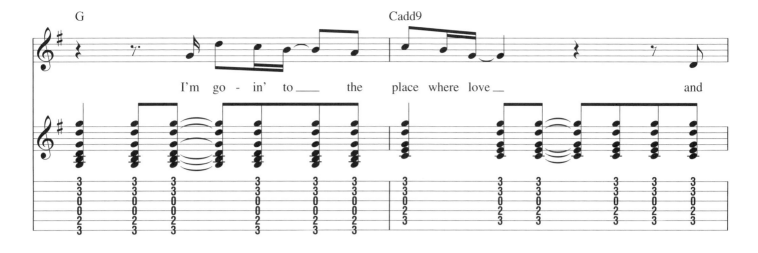

I'm go - in' to _____ the place where love _____ and

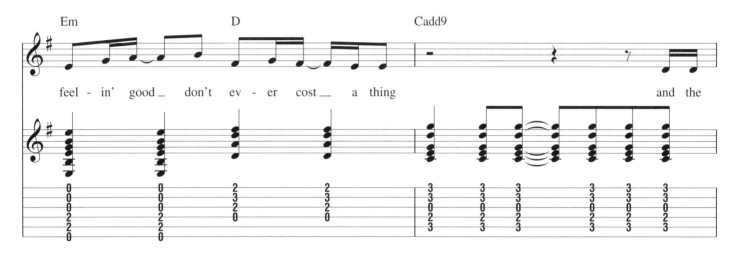

feel - in' good _ don't ev - er cost _ a thing and the

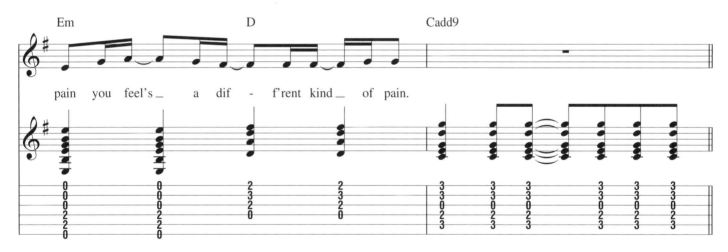

pain you feel's _ a dif - f'rent kind _ of pain.

𝄋 Chorus

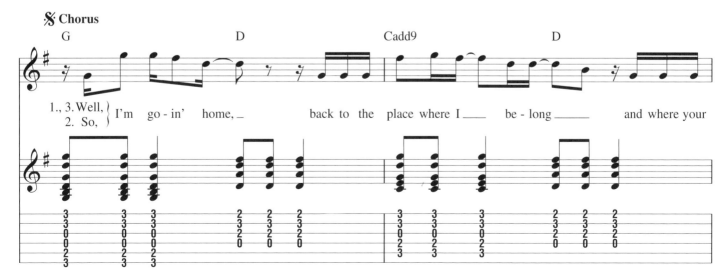

1., 3. Well,
2. So, } I'm go - in' home, _ back to the place where I _____ be - long _____ and where your

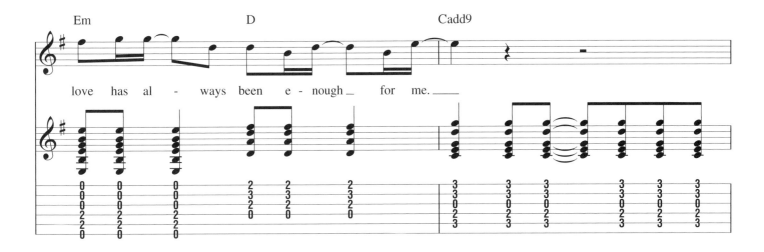

love has al - ways been e - nough __ for me. __

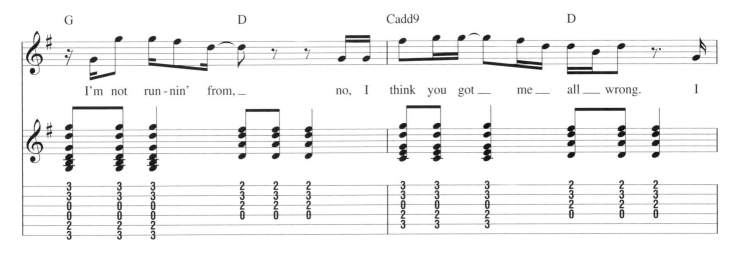

I'm not run - nin' from, __ no, I think you got __ me __ all __ wrong. I

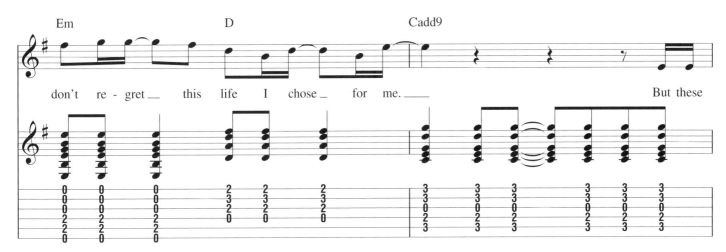

don't re - gret __ this life I chose __ for me. __ But these

To Coda ⊕

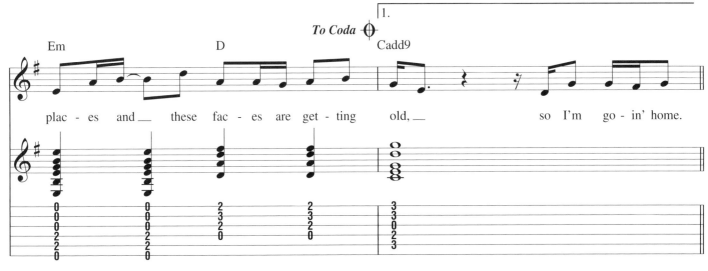

plac - es and __ these fac - es are get - ting old, __ so I'm go - in' home.

Interlude

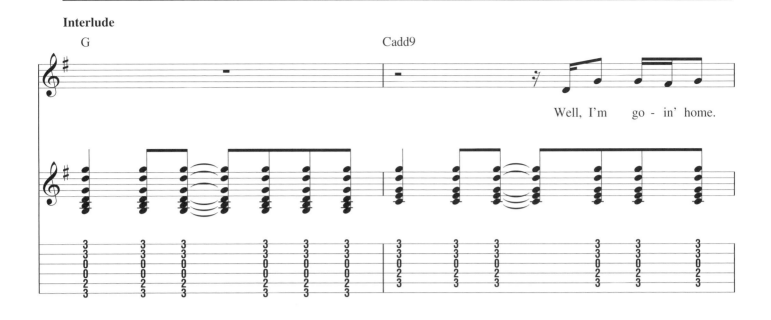

Well, I'm go-in' home.

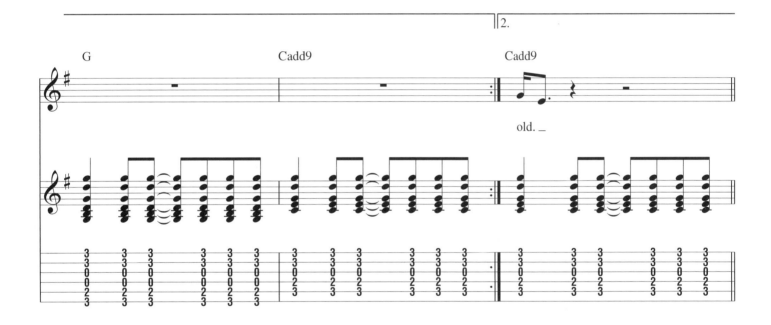

old. ___

Bridge

Be care-ful what ___ you wish for ___ 'cause you just might get it all. ___

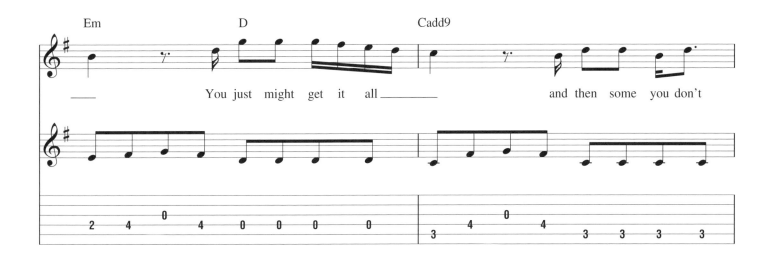

You just might get it all _____ and then some you don't

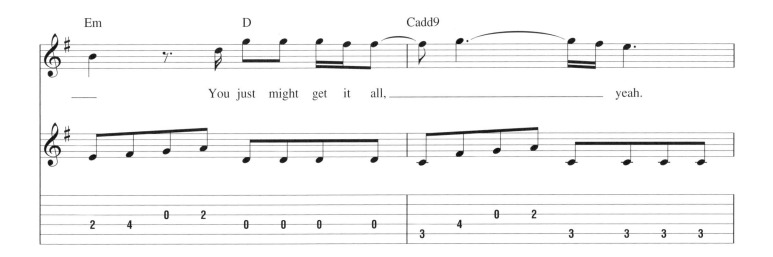

want. __ Be care - ful what _ you wish for ____ 'cause you just might get it all. __

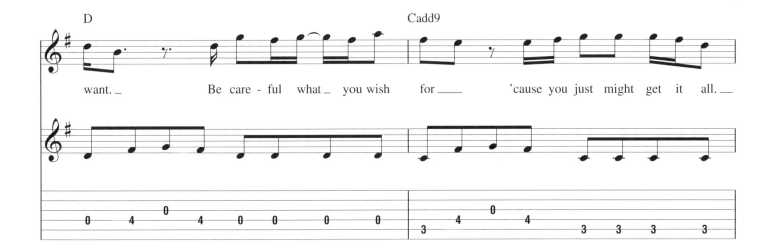

You just might get it all, _____ yeah.

D.S. al Coda

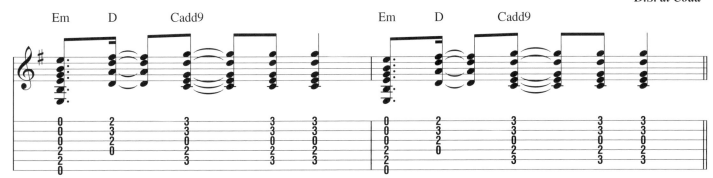

⊕ Coda

old. ___   I said, these plac - es and ___ these fac - es are get - ting

old, ___   so I'm go - in' home. _____

I'm go - in' home. _____

Additional Lyrics

2. The miles are getting longer, it seems,
   The closer I get to you.
   I've not always been the best man or friend for you,
   But your love remains true.
   And I don't know why
   You always seem to give me another try.

◆ ⑧ Use Somebody

Words and Music by Caleb Followill, Nathan Followill, Jared Followill and Matthew Followill

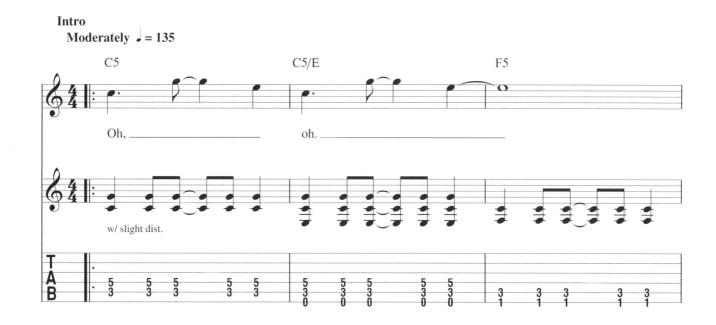

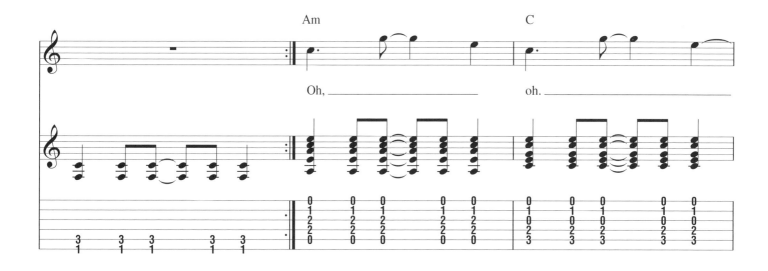

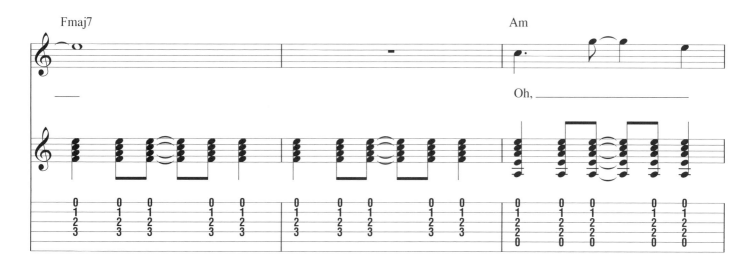

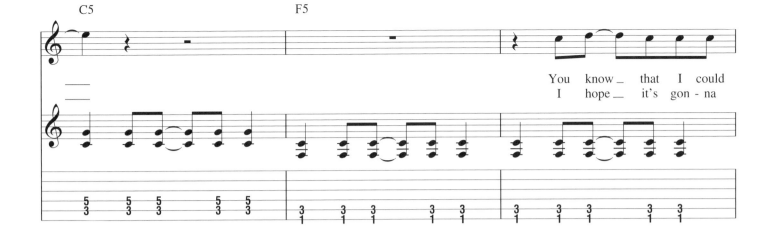

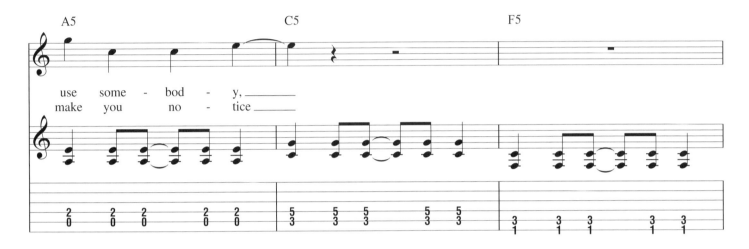

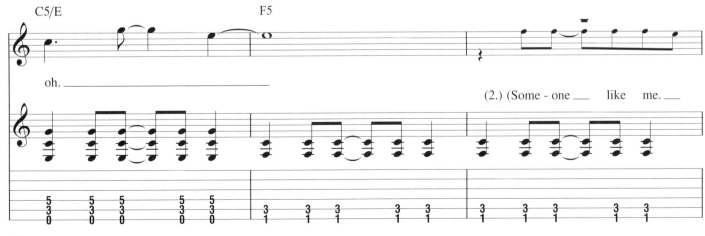

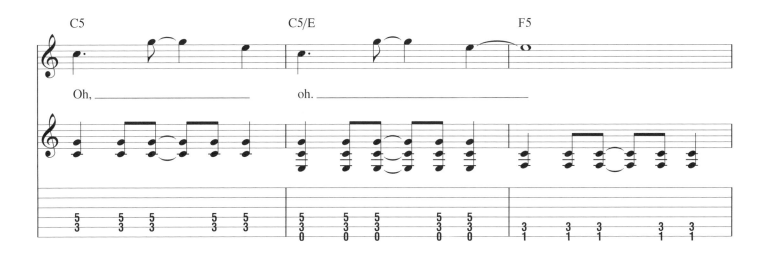

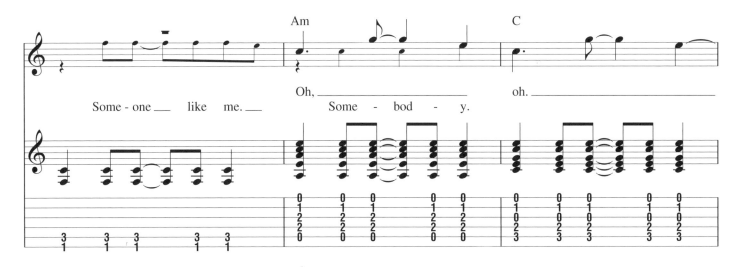

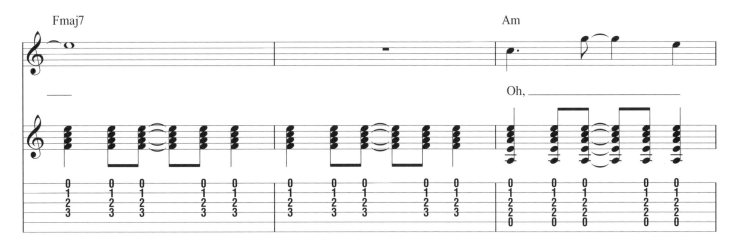

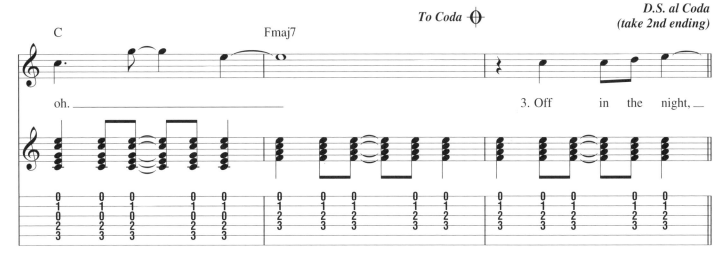

Coda

Bridge

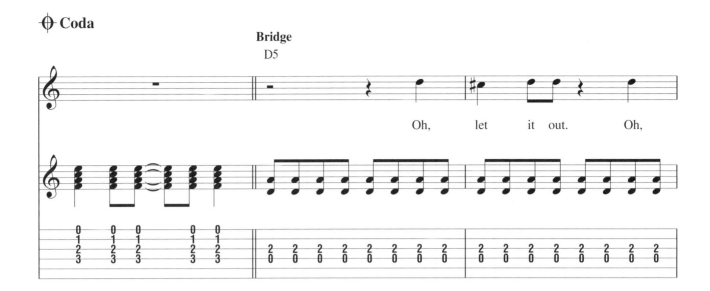

D5

Oh, let it out. Oh,

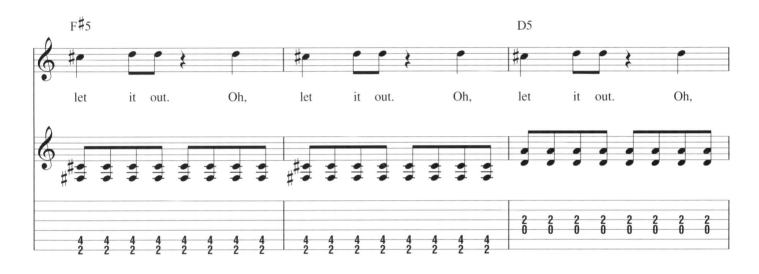

F♯5
D5

let it out. Oh, let it out. Oh, let it out. Oh,

F♯5
B5 **N.C.**

let it out. Oh, let it out. Oh, let it out.

Guitar Solo

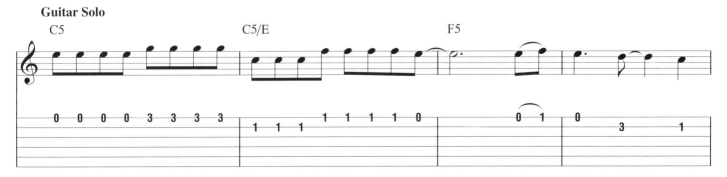

C5 **C5/E** **F5**

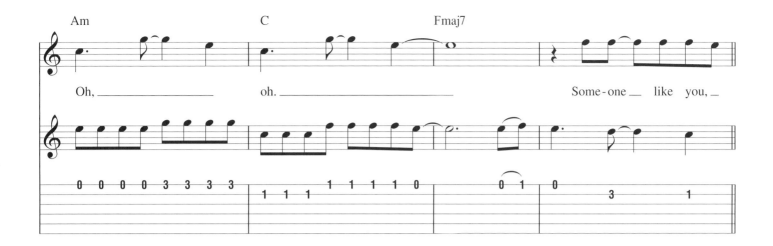

Oh, _____ oh. _____ Some-one ___ like you, _

Chorus

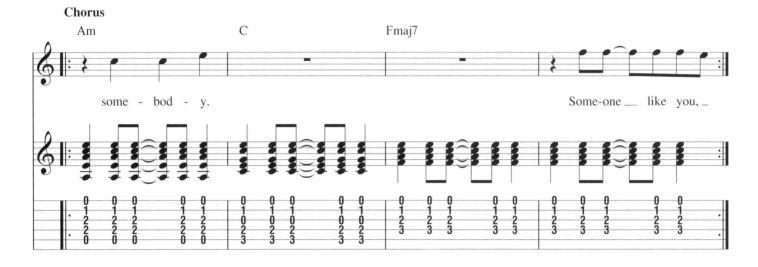

some - bod - y. Some-one ___ like you, _

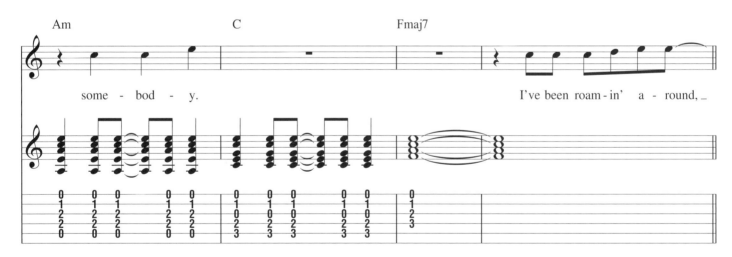

some - bod - y. I've been roam - in' a - round, _

Outro

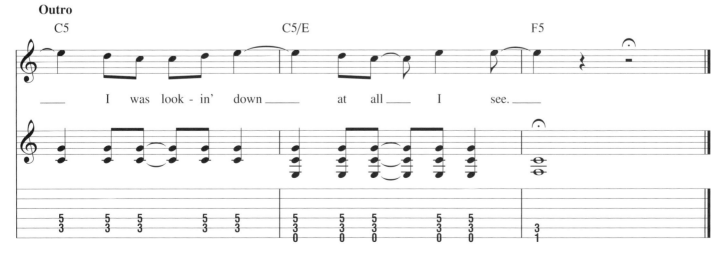

_____ I was look - in' down _____ at all ___ I see. _

21 Guns

Words and Music by David Bowie, John Phillips, Billie Joe Armstrong, Mike Pritchard and Frank Wright

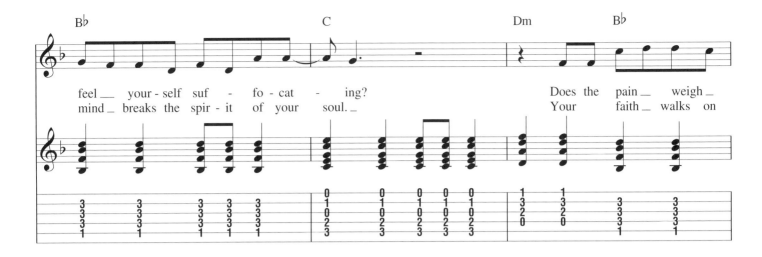

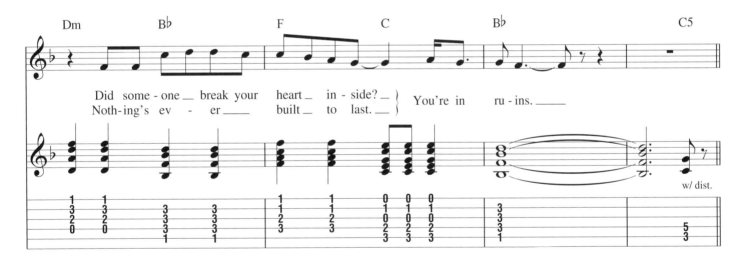

𝄋 Chorus

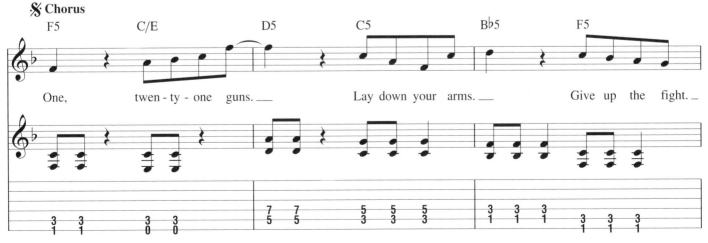

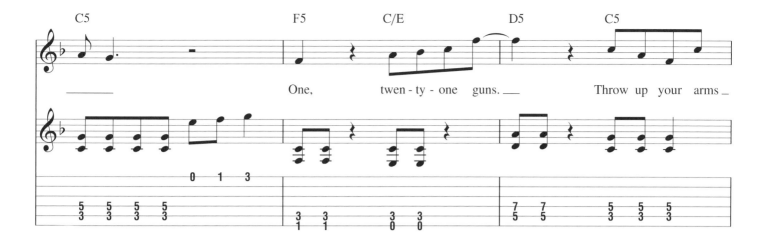

One, twen-ty-one guns. ___ Throw up your arms ___

To Coda ⊕

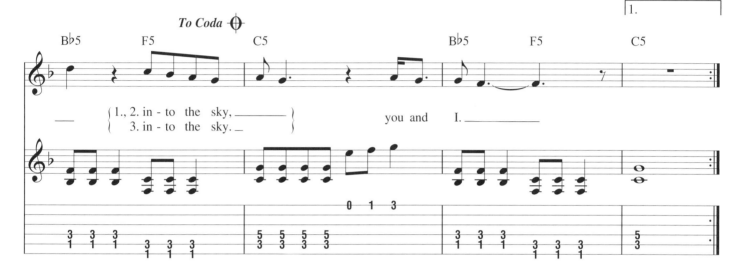

___ { 1., 2. in-to the sky, ___ }
{ 3. in-to the sky. ___ }
you and I. ___

1.

2.

Bridge

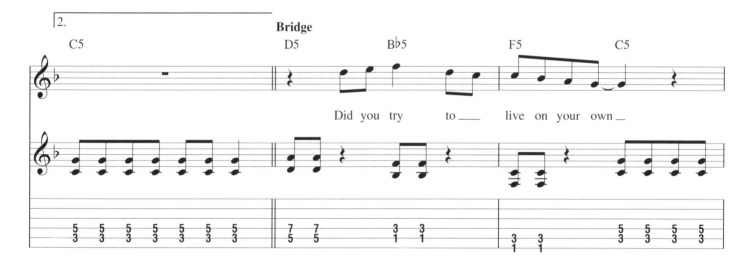

Did you try to ___ live on your own ___

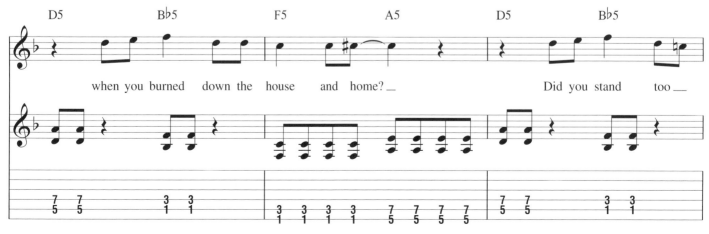

when you burned down the house and home? ___ Did you stand too ___

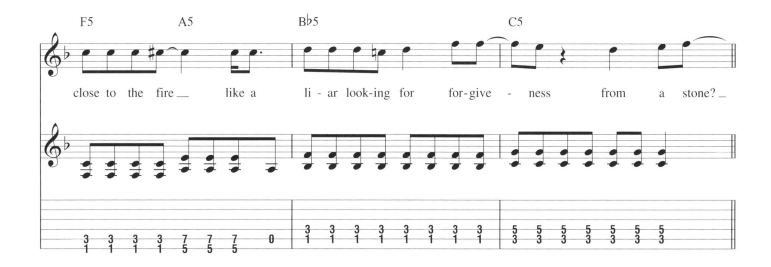

close to the fire ___ like a li - ar look-ing for for-give - ness from a stone? ___

Guitar Solo

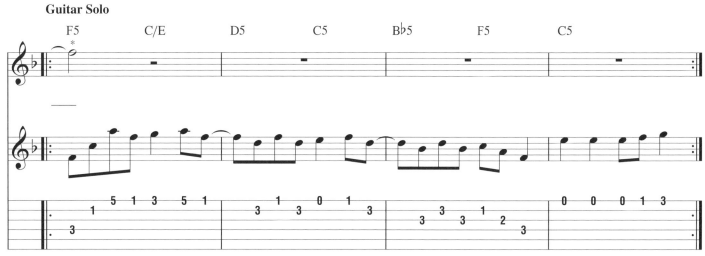

*Sing 1st time only.

Interlude

w/ clean tone

Verse

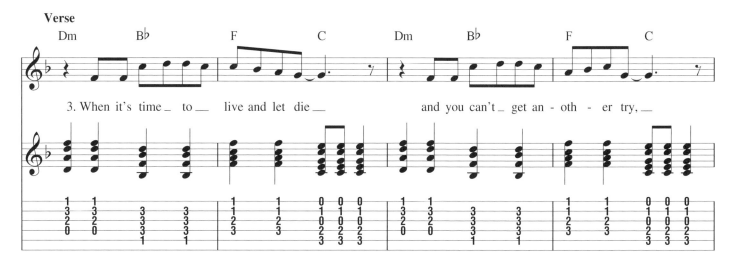

3. When it's time ___ to ___ live and let die ___ and you can't ___ get an - oth - er try, ___

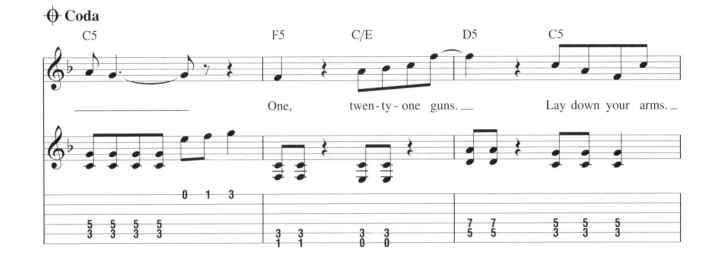

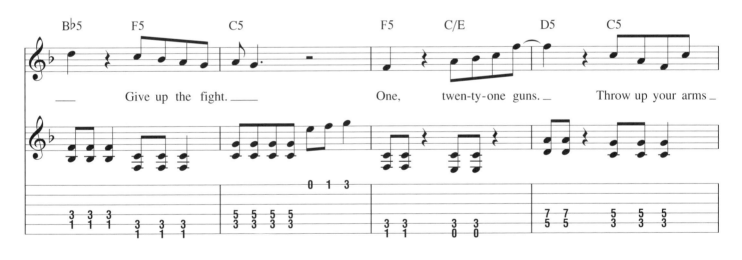

FastTrack is the fastest way for beginners to learn to play the instrument they just bought. FastTrack is different from other method books: we've made our book/CD packs user-friendly with plenty of cool songs that make it easy and fun for players to teach themselves. Plus, the last section of the FastTrack books have the same songs so that students can form a band and jam together. Songbooks for Guitar, Bass, Keyboard and Drums are all compatible, and feature eight songs including hits such as Wild Thing • Twist and Shout • Layla • Born to Be Wild • and more! All packs include a great play-along CD with a professional-sounding back-up band.

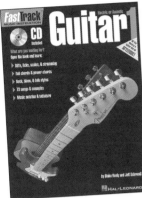

FASTTRACK GUITAR

For Electric or Acoustic Guitar – or both!
by Blake Neely & Jeff Schroedl
Book/CD Packs

Teaches music notation, tablature, full chords and power chords, riffs, licks, scales, and rock and blues styles. Method Book 1 includes 73 songs and examples.

LEVEL 1
00697282	Method Book – 9" x 12"	$7.99
00695390	Method Book – 5½" x 5"	$7.95
00697287	Songbook 1 – 9" x 12"	$12.95
00695397	Songbook 1 – 5½" x 5"	$9.95
00695343	Songbook 2	$12.95
00696438	Rock Songbook 1	$12.99
00696057	DVD	$7.99

LEVEL 2
00697286	Method Book	$9.99
00697296	Songbook 1	$12.95
00695344	Songbook 2	$12.95

CHORDS & SCALES
00697291	9" x 12"	$9.95
00696588	Spanish Edition	$9.99

FASTTRACK BASS

by Blake Neely & Jeff Schroedl
Book/CD Packs

Everything you need to know about playing the bass, including music notation, tablature, riffs, licks, scales, syncopation, and rock and blues styles. Method Book 1 includes 75 songs and examples.

LEVEL 1
00697284	Method Book – 9" x 12"	$7.95
00697289	Songbook 1 – 9" x 12"	$12.95
00695400	Songbook 1 – 5½" x 5"	$9.95
00695368	Songbook 2	$12.95
00696440	Rock Songbook 1	$12.99
00696058	DVD	$7.99

LEVEL 2
00697294	Method Book	$9.95
00697298	Songbook 1	$12.95
00695369	Songbook 2	$12.95

FASTTRACK KEYBOARD

For Electric Keyboard, Synthesizer, or Piano
by Blake Neely & Gary Meisner
Book/CD Packs

Learn how to play that piano today! With this book you'll learn music notation, chords, riffs, licks, scales, syncopation, and rock and blues styles. Method Book 1 includes over 87 songs and examples.

LEVEL 1
00697283	Method Book – 9" x 12"	$7.99
00697288	Songbook 1 – 9" x 12"	$12.95
00695366	Songbook 2	$12.95
00696439	Rock Songbook 1	$12.99
00696060	DVD	$7.99

LEVEL 2
00697293	Method Book	$9.95
00697297	Songbook 1	$12.95
00695370	Songbook 2	$12.99

CHORDS & SCALES
00697292	9" x 12"	$9.95

FASTTRACK DRUM

by Blake Neely & Rick Mattingly
Book/CD Packs

With this book, you'll learn music notation, riffs and licks, syncopation, rock, blues and funk styles, and improvisation. Method Book 1 includes over 75 songs and examples.

LEVEL 1
00697285	Method Book – 9" x 12"	$7.95
00695396	Method Book – 5½" x 5"	$7.95
00697290	Songbook 1 – 9" x 12"	$12.95
00695367	Songbook 2	$12.95
00696441	Rock Songbook 1	$12.99

LEVEL 2
00697295	Method Book	$9.95
00697299	Songbook 1	$12.95
00695371	Songbook 2	$12.95
00696059	DVD	$7.99

FASTTRACK SAXOPHONE

by Blake Neely
Book/CD Packs

With this book, you'll learn music notation; riffs, scales, keys; syncopation; rock and blues styles; and more. Includes 72 songs and examples.

LEVEL 1
00695241	Method Book	$7.95
00695409	Songbook	$12.95

FASTTRACK HARMONICA

by Blake Neely & Doug Downing
Book/CD Packs

These books cover all you need to learn C Diatonic harmonica, including: music notation • singles notes and chords • riffs, licks & scales • syncopation • rock and blues styles. Method Book 1 includes over 70 songs and examples.

LEVEL 1
00695407	Method Book	$7.99
00695574	Songbook	$12.95

LEVEL 2
00695889	Method Book	$9.95

FASTTRACK LEAD SINGER

by Blake Neely
Book/CD Packs

Everything you need to be a great singer, including: how to read music, microphone tips, warm-up exercises, ear training, syncopation, and more. Method Book 1 includes 80 songs and examples.

LEVEL 1
00695408	Method Book	$7.99
00695410	Songbook	$12.95
00696589	Spanish Edition	$7.99

LEVEL 2
00695892	Songbook 1	$12.95

FOR MORE INFORMATION, SEE YOUR LOCAL MUSIC DEALER,
OR WRITE TO:

HAL•LEONARD® CORPORATION

7777 W. BLUEMOUND RD. P.O. BOX 13819 MILWAUKEE, WI 53213

Visit Hal Leonard online at **www.halleonard.com**

HAL•LEONARD GUITAR PLAY•ALONG®

This series will help you play your favorite songs quickly and easily. Just follow the tab and listen to the CD to the hear how the guitar should sound, and then play along using the separate backing tracks. Mac or PC users can also slow down the tempo without changing pitch by using the CD in their computer. The melody and lyrics are included in the book so that you can sing or simply follow along.

INCLUDES TAB

VOL. 1 – ROCK	00699570 / $16.99	
VOL. 2 – ACOUSTIC	00699569 / $16.95	
VOL. 3 – HARD ROCK	00699573 / $16.95	
VOL. 4 – POP/ROCK	00699571 / $16.99	
VOL. 5 – MODERN ROCK	00699574 / $16.99	
VOL. 6 – '90s ROCK	00699572 / $16.99	
VOL. 7 – BLUES	00699575 / $16.95	
VOL. 8 – ROCK	00699585 / $14.99	
VOL. 9 – PUNK ROCK	00699576 / $14.95	
VOL. 10 – ACOUSTIC	00699586 / $16.95	
VOL. 11 – EARLY ROCK	00699579 / $14.95	
VOL. 12 – POP/ROCK	00699587 / $14.95	
VOL. 13 – FOLK ROCK	00699581 / $14.95	
VOL. 14 – BLUES ROCK	00699582 / $16.95	
VOL. 15 – R&B	00699583 / $14.95	
VOL. 16 – JAZZ	00699584 / $15.95	
VOL. 17 – COUNTRY	00699588 / $15.95	
VOL. 18 – ACOUSTIC ROCK	00699577 / $15.95	
VOL. 19 – SOUL	00699578 / $14.99	
VOL. 20 – ROCKABILLY	00699580 / $14.95	
VOL. 21 – YULETIDE	00699602 / $14.95	
VOL. 22 – CHRISTMAS	00699600 / $15.95	
VOL. 23 – SURF	00699635 / $14.95	
VOL. 24 – ERIC CLAPTON	00699649 / $17.99	
VOL. 25 – LENNON & McCARTNEY	00699642 / $16.99	
VOL. 26 – ELVIS PRESLEY	00699643 / $14.95	
VOL. 27 – DAVID LEE ROTH	00699645 / $16.95	
VOL. 28 – GREG KOCH	00699646 / $14.95	
VOL. 29 – BOB SEGER	00699647 / $15.99	
VOL. 30 – KISS	00699644 / $16.99	
VOL. 31 – CHRISTMAS HITS	00699652 / $14.95	
VOL. 32 – THE OFFSPRING	00699653 / $14.95	
VOL. 33 – ACOUSTIC CLASSICS	00699656 / $16.95	
VOL. 34 – CLASSIC ROCK	00699658 / $16.95	
VOL. 35 – HAIR METAL	00699660 / $16.95	
VOL. 36 – SOUTHERN ROCK	00699661 / $16.95	
VOL. 37 – ACOUSTIC METAL	00699662 / $16.95	
VOL. 38 – BLUES	00699663 / $16.95	
VOL. 39 – '80s METAL	00699664 / $16.99	
VOL. 40 – INCUBUS	00699668 / $17.95	
VOL. 41 – ERIC CLAPTON	00699669 / $16.95	
VOL. 42 – 2000s ROCK	00699670 / $16.99	
VOL. 43 – LYNYRD SKYNYRD	00699681 / $17.95	
VOL. 44 – JAZZ	00699689 / $14.99	
VOL. 45 – TV THEMES	00699718 / $14.95	
VOL. 46 – MAINSTREAM ROCK	00699722 / $16.95	
VOL. 47 – HENDRIX SMASH HITS	00699723 / $19.95	
VOL. 48 – AEROSMITH CLASSICS	00699724 / $17.99	

VOL. 49 – STEVIE RAY VAUGHAN	00699725 / $17.99
VOL. 50 – 2000s METAL	00699726 / $16.99
VOL. 51 – ALTERNATIVE '90s	00699727 / $12.95
VOL. 52 – FUNK	00699728 / $14.95
VOL. 53 – DISCO	00699729 / $14.99
VOL. 54 – HEAVY METAL	00699730 / $14.95
VOL. 55 – POP METAL	00699731 / $14.95
VOL. 56 – FOO FIGHTERS	00699749 / $14.95
VOL. 57 – SYSTEM OF A DOWN	00699751 / $14.95
VOL. 58 – BLINK-182	00699772 / $14.95
VOL. 60 – 3 DOORS DOWN	00699774 / $14.95
VOL. 61 – SLIPKNOT	00699775 / $14.95
VOL. 62 – CHRISTMAS CAROLS	00699798 / $12.95
VOL. 63 – CREEDENCE CLEARWATER REVIVAL	00699802 / $16.99
VOL. 64 – THE ULTIMATE OZZY OSBOURNE	00699803 / $16.99
VOL. 65 – THE DOORS	00699806 / $16.99
VOL. 66 – THE ROLLING STONES	00699807 / $16.95
VOL. 67 – BLACK SABBATH	00699808 / $16.99
VOL. 68 – PINK FLOYD – DARK SIDE OF THE MOON	00699809 / $16.99
VOL. 69 – ACOUSTIC FAVORITES	00699810 / $14.95
VOL. 70 – OZZY OSBOURNE	00699805 / $16.99
VOL. 71 – CHRISTIAN ROCK	00699824 / $14.95
VOL. 72 – ACOUSTIC '90s	00699827 / $14.95
VOL. 73 – BLUESY ROCK	00699829 / $16.99
VOL. 74 – PAUL BALOCHE	00699831 / $14.95
VOL. 75 – TOM PETTY	00699882 / $16.99
VOL. 76 – COUNTRY HITS	00699884 / $14.95
VOL. 77 – BLUEGRASS	00699910 / $12.99
VOL. 78 – NIRVANA	00700132 / $16.99
VOL. 80 – ACOUSTIC ANTHOLOGY	00700175 / $19.95
VOL. 81 – ROCK ANTHOLOGY	00700176 / $22.99
VOL. 82 – EASY SONGS	00700177 / $12.99
VOL. 83 – THREE CHORD SONGS	00700178 / $16.99
VOL. 84 – STEELY DAN	00700200 / $16.99
VOL. 85 – THE POLICE	00700269 /$16.99
VOL. 86 – BOSTON	00700465 / $16.99
VOL. 87 – ACOUSTIC WOMEN	00700763 / $14.99
VOL. 88 – GRUNGE	00700467 / $16.99
VOL. 90 – CLASSICAL POP	00700469 / $12.99
VOL. 91 – BLUES INSTRUMENTALS	00700505 / $14.99
VOL. 92 – EARLY ROCK INSTRUMENTALS	00700506 / $12.99
VOL. 93 – ROCK INSTRUMENTALS	00700507 / $16.99
VOL. 95 – BLUES CLASSICS	00700509 / $14.99
VOL. 96 – THIRD DAY	00700560 / $14.95
VOL. 97 – ROCK BAND	00700703 / $14.99
VOL. 98 – ROCK BAND	00700704 / $14.95
VOL. 99 – ZZ TOP	00700762 / $16.99

VOL. 100 – B.B. KING	00700466 / $16.99
VOL. 101 – SONGS FOR BEGINNERS	00701917 / $14.99
VOL. 102 – CLASSIC PUNK	00700769 / $14.99
VOL. 103 – SWITCHFOOT	00700773 / $16.99
VOL. 104 – DUANE ALLMAN	00700846 / $16.99
VOL. 106 – WEEZER	00700958 / $14.99
VOL. 107 – CREAM	00701069 / $16.99
VOL. 108 – THE WHO	00701053 / $16.99
VOL. 109 – STEVE MILLER	00701054 / $14.99
VOL. 111 – JOHN MELLENCAMP	00701056 / $14.99
VOL. 112 – QUEEN	00701052 / $16.99
VOL. 113 – JIM CROCE	00701058 / $14.99
VOL. 114 – BON JOVI	00701060 / $14.99
VOL. 115 – JOHNNY CASH	00701070 / $16.99
VOL. 116 – THE VENTURES	00701124 / $14.99
VOL. 119 – AC/DC CLASSICS	00701356 / $17.99
VOL. 120 – PROGRESSIVE ROCK	00701457 / $14.99
VOL. 121 – U2	00701508 / $16.99
VOL. 122 – CROSBY, STILLS & NASH	00701610 / $16.99
VOL. 123 – LENNON & McCARTNEY ACOUSTIC	00701614 / $16.99
VOL. 124 – MODERN WORSHIP	00701629 / $14.99
VOL. 125 – JEFF BECK	00701687 / $16.99
VOL. 126 – BOB MARLEY	00701701 / $16.99
VOL. 127 – 1970s ROCK	00701739 / $14.99
VOL. 128 – 1960s ROCK	00701740 / $14.99
VOL. 129 – MEGADETH	00701741 / $14.99
VOL. 130 – IRON MAIDEN	00701742 / $14.99
VOL. 131 – 1990s ROCK	00701743 / $14.99
VOL. 132 – COUNTRY ROCK	00701757 / $14.99
VOL. 133 – TAYLOR SWIFT	00701894 / $16.99
VOL. 134 – AVENGED SEVENFOLD	00701906 / $16.99
VOL. 136 – GUITAR THEMES	00701922 / $14.99
VOL. 139 – GARY MOORE	00702370 / $16.99
VOL. 141 – ACOUSTIC HITS	00702401 / $16.99
VOL. 142 – KINGS OF LEON	00702418 / $16.99
VOL. 145 – DEF LEPPARD	00702532 / $16.99
VOL. 149 – AC/DC HITS	14041593 / $17.99

Complete song lists available online.

Prices, contents, and availability subject to change without notice.

HAL•LEONARD® CORPORATION

7777 W. BLUEMOUND RD. P.O. BOX 13819 MILWAUKEE, WI 53213

Visit Hal Leonard online at
www.halleonard.com